CONTENTS

THE BIG SCREEN

I was shopping on Black Friday—which was probably a mistake.

As I jostled with the crowds in search of a bargain, my eyes were drawn to the TV section at the back of the store. And what I noticed was that nearly all of the TVs on sale were giant in size. Anything under sixty inches is hardly worth having these days, it seems.

I do not know what type of screen you most like to watch a movie on. Certainly the size of the screen impacts your experience. There is a convenience to watching something on your phone. Sometimes the new sixty-inch TV in your living room is great. Of course, thousands enjoy the big-screen experience of the cinema.

And then there is the *really* big screen—the IMAX dome—if you're looking for the full, immersive experience.

Sometimes it's wonderful to look at the Christmas story on the small screen and see the more intimate moments: Mary and Joseph traveling to Bethlehem, the baby in the manger, and the shepherds in the field. But there is also value in approaching the story through a wider lens.

One of the accounts of Jesus' life in the Bible is written by his disciple, John. He chose the largest screen imaginable to tell the story of Jesus' birth. John gives us the cosmic perspective, as if on the ultimate IMAX screen. The scene opens before the universe even existed: "In the beginning was the Word, and the Word was with God, and the Word was God" (John 1:1).

John does not begin his Christmas story with the angel's visit to Mary, or the star over Bethlehem, or the manger in a stable. No, he starts at the *very* beginning, further back in time than we can imagine. Before the world even existed (let alone stables and mangers), Jesus was there. John wants to show us that Jesus is more than an influential teacher or a wise guide.

He's more than a good man or an example for others. Jesus is unique in all the universe. There is no one like him.

Are you searching for something this Christmas? Perhaps, like so many, you're seeking meaning or peace or hope. Maybe you just sense there might be something in Jesus worth considering. If so, John invites you to sit back and experience the impact of the real Christmas story on the big screen; events which begin before time and connect all the way through to our lives here and now, this Christmas.

THE LIGHT THAT SHATTERS DARKNESS

In the beginning was the Word, and the Word was with God, and the Word was God. He was in the beginning with God. All things were made through him, and without him was not any thing made that was made. In him was life, and the life was the light of men. The light shines in the darkness, and the darkness has not overcome it (John 1:1–5).

Words are powerful things. When I speak, I convey something of myself—my thoughts, my feelings, my identity. When you speak, you do the same.

Words have the power to make things happen. I can drive up to the window at Starbucks and speak into the microphone, asking for a grande peppermint mocha with extra whip. When I drive round the corner, I discover that my words have had a real effect as I am handed my coffee and the credit card machine.

I can speak words of encouragement and transform someone's day. I can speak words of criticism and see someone crumble. We see the power of words whenever we speak to Siri or Alexa; ask for the forecast, directions, or music, and they immediately oblige.

If, even as finite human beings, our words can be relatively powerful, imagine the impact of the words of a supremely powerful God. The Bible is clear on this:

> By the word of the LORD the heavens were made,
>   and by the breath of his mouth all their host.
>   (Psalm 33:6)

The word of God goes out from his mouth and things happen. The heavens appear. Stars are made.

As John introduces us to the Son of God at the beginning of his Gospel, he calls him "the Word." John puts Jesus Christ into the same category as the powerful word of God.

*

"In the beginning was the Word and the Word was with God."

The baby born in a Bethlehem stable and placed in a manger was and is the Word of God—the powerful walking, talking Word by which God made the world and does his work. In the beginning this Word of God simply *was*, which means there has never been a time when he did not exist. Right from the start, he was "with" God.

There is a distinction here between God the Father and "the Word." The Word of God is not simply an idea, or a principle, or a message from the ether. He is a person. But as well as being "with" God, the Word of God "was" God. "In the beginning was the Word and the Word was *with* God, and the Word *was* God" (my emphasis). God the Son—the Word—is united to God the Father in oneness. We aren't talking about two gods here. No, the Bible makes it clear that there is one true God, and people came face to face with him in Jesus as he lay in the manger.

It is very easy to domesticate Jesus at Christmastime. The image of a baby in a manger is a tender and vulnerable one. And that's right. It is meant to be. But we must not underestimate or misunderstand this child. The Word of God who came into the world is the eternal Word, the one who was with God at the beginning and the one who is God himself.

The child of Christmas is not feebly crying out for your attention from a manger of straw, longing and hoping that you might notice him. Not at all. He is the eternal God, the Lord of heaven and earth. He is the very Word of God and the embodiment of God's own message to the world.

*

I was at a friend's house recently and he took me on a tour of the workshop in his basement. Let me tell you that if you are someone who likes woodwork, this is a place of wonder and delight. He designed the workshop himself. He built the walls and the workbenches. He sealed the room and set up an air filtration system.

Now, my friend and his wife keep their home to a beautiful standard. You would be hard-pressed to find a speck of dust anywhere upstairs. But the workshop is a separate zone. The workshop is *his* room. Dust and tools and half-finished projects (and the mess that goes with them), well, they are allowed in there. He made the workshop and so he makes the rules.

The opening of John's Gospel makes a simple but profound claim about Jesus Christ: "All things were made through him, and without him was not any thing made that was made." God the Father and God the Son co-operated in the work of creation. God the Son carried out the work of bringing creation into being. And so we have to say that the universe rightfully belongs to Jesus because, like my friend's workshop, it is his creation.

We humans can make things. When we do, we know how to claim them as our own. We make a workshop in the basement—it is our special place. We build a house or a cottage—maybe if we are ambitious, we build something larger—and when we enter the place we have made, we feel a sense of ownership and know our rights.

Jesus entered our world not as a salesman vying for our attention, but as the designer, the owner, the creator, claiming that which belongs to him.

In the marketplace of ideas, where the philosophies and religions of this world shout for our attention, a baby lying in the straw might not seem very impressive. But the gentleness and grace of Jesus must not be mistaken for powerlessness or irrelevance. He is the mighty creator of all things—of this world, of me, of you.

*

One Saturday morning my family's phone was ringing at a very unsociable hour. I jumped out of bed imagining that it was some kind of emergency. I couldn't think why anyone would call so early on a Saturday. Of course, it turned out to be one of those scam calls, where they try and trick you into giving away personal financial information.

Millions are lost to phone scams each year. You have probably received some of these calls yourself. Someone phones up claiming to be a representative of the bank, asking for information or money from you. We have come to learn that these calls are fraudulent and that the people at the end of the phone have no claim on us or our money. To be sure, if they were truly representatives from the bank, they would have a rightful claim on our time. But unless they can prove they are legitimate, they have no claim at all.

Jesus Christ calls for more than just a few minutes of our time. He asks us to turn from living for ourselves, and to live for God instead. If we continue reading in John's Gospel, even just the opening few chapters, we see that Jesus calls people to follow him in obedience and faith.

He issues the same call today. But many people view it as little better than a fraudulent bank call— just another scam, just another manipulation.

"What claim does Jesus have on my life?" we say. But to respond in that way means we have not understood the beginning of John's Gospel and the truth that all things were made through Jesus. The world is, if you like, his basement workshop, and you and I are part of his creation. We belong to him. We owe our very existence to him. He is perfectly within his rights to claim us. His call is a legitimate one.

His call is also a profoundly positive one for us. This Christmas, the invitation to you is not simply to be reminded of a baby in a manger, but to meet him. To meet the one who made you and this world, and to whom you owe your very life. To meet the one who brings the light we so desperately need in our lives.

*

It is tragic to say this, but I think we all know it's true: the world is a dark place.

Do not misunderstand me—there is plenty that is good and pleasant in the world. But there is a heavy darkness casting its shadow over all that we experience, even during the Christmas season.

I like to try and keep on top of the news. I have a couple of news outlets that I follow regularly. But it is rarely uplifting to go through the newsfeed in the morning. Sure, there are those occasional rays of light, but mostly it is just different shades of darkness.

Despite the beauty of the creation and the warmth of human relationships, the world is sorely damaged by sin. The Bible tells us that when God created humanity by his Word, people lived in the light of his presence and experienced his life—a life that would never need to fade or end. But the first humans began to doubt God's goodness and refused to live under his gracious rule. In response to that, God sent them out of his life-giving presence and into a world now broken and tainted by sin. Because humanity turned against its maker right back in the Garden of Eden, we all now experience the devastating consequences of humanity's choice to live without reference to God.

We see the implications of this at every turn—in illness, in poverty, in injustice, and in natural disasters. We feel the darkness as we navigate an ethical landscape that has become so confused that, as a society, we can hardly agree anymore on the difference between right and wrong. We feel the darkness as we confront the tragedy of death, which is never far from our experience. All this drives home the reality that we are living in a profoundly broken world. We need God's light.

*

In Canada, where I live, it is not unusual to find yourself stuck in a snowstorm. I remember driving home one evening when a very dramatic snow squall came up. The snow was blowing in sideways with a powerful wind for about half an hour. For me it was one of the few occasions when I quite literally could not see the road and could barely see the car in front. It was scary and made driving really quite dangerous. Occasionally as I crawled along, a big truck with powerful headlights would approach from the opposite direction, and its lights would penetrate the blizzard for a moment or two. When I came to an intersection with good street lights shining above, then I could see for a bit, at least while I passed through that place. The only thing that helped with the driving was the intermittent appearance of powerful light, but on my route out of town such lights were few and far between.

The true light of the one and only God has been shining in his creation since the beginning of time. It shines in the natural world that he has made, despite the brokenness of creation. The Bible tells us that the eternal God has made himself known in and through his creation in a general way. But what we discover from reading John's Gospel is that the great, true light—the light of lights that gives light to all people—

has come into the world. He came that first Christmas to give us deeper, brighter knowledge. The light came among us that we might know him, understand him, respond to him, and enjoy the light he brings to our lives.

"In him was life, and the life was the light of men. The light shines in the darkness, and the darkness has not overcome it," writes John. When Jesus was born, a bright star marked out the place of his birth. Just as the light of the star shone in the darkness of the night sky that first Christmas, so the light of the Word shines in the darkness of the world. It is by his inextinguishable light that we can truly know our creator and confidently navigate our journey through life.

THE LIGHT THAT SHINES ON US

The true light, which gives light to everyone, was coming into the world. He was in the world, and the world was made through him, yet the world did not know him. He came to his own, and his own people did not receive him. But to all who did receive him, who believed in his name, he gave the right to become children of God, who were born, not of blood nor of the will of the flesh nor of the will of man, but of God (John 1:9–13).

I have heard a number of stories about people who have inherited property abroad. Because the property is overseas, it is left empty for a long time, or is perhaps in the care of a distant family member. But the day comes when they decide to visit their home, perhaps with the aim of fixing it up and making something of it. After a long journey they arrive at the property, only to discover that squatters or opportunists have taken it over and have made it their own. And now, in what should be a special family place, the children and grandchildren are unwelcome. It is made clear that they are not wanted there and the inheritance will not be given over to them easily.

When Jesus Christ arrived, the initial reaction of the world was far from welcoming: "He was in the world, and the world was made through him, yet the world did not know him. He came to his own, and his own people did not receive him." As we saw in the previous chapter, the universe belongs to Jesus. He is, in fact, the one through whom the world was made. But when he came into this world, the world did not know him or recognize him.

*

There is no doubt that goodness shone through everything Jesus said and did. His words were filled with kindness and grace. His actions overflowed with integrity and love. His interactions were marked by compassion and care. He reached out to those on the margins of society and welcomed the outcast. He touched those deemed unclean. He treated women with respect in a society where they were often sidelined. He gave attention to children at a time when others ignored them. He showed grace to the sinful, the disliked, and the disreputable. He healed the sick and cast out demons. He preached the good news of salvation and offered freely the forgiveness of sins.

This was a life that radiated the pure light of God's own goodness and grace. In Jesus, the healing, restoring, life-giving presence of the creator God himself was in the world. But the world was largely unimpressed. People neither knew nor accepted him. In particular, his "own people"—presumably referring to the people of Israel, because Jesus was an Israelite—rejected him.

Jesus came, in the first instance, as the Messiah of Israel. He came in fulfilment of the promises of the Old Testament Scriptures. But even within Israel, where there was a hopeful expectation of the Messiah's arrival—of a promised Savior to come—Jesus was not received.

Why was the light of the world not recognized when he came into the darkness? That is an important question for us to consider. The widespread rejection of Jesus Christ was a reality from his birth, through his life on earth to his death, and it is even the reality today. That is not to say that *no one* accepted him, but we can hardly ignore the fact that the majority in our society reject him even now.

When we probe this question a little from the Bible, I think we are given two answers.

The first reason that many reject the light of the world is that human beings naturally like the darkness. Jesus himself tells us this a little later in John's Gospel:

And this is the judgment: the light has come into the world, and people loved the darkness rather than the light because their works were evil. For everyone who does wicked things hates the light and does not come to the light, lest his works should be exposed (John 3:19–20).

Why would anyone reject light in favor of darkness? Why would anyone choose to stay in the shadowy gloom when they could step into the radiant brightness? Jesus says people love darkness because the darkness is a better home—a more suitable environment—for their evil deeds.

*

Just after 3am on 8 August 1963, a mail train heading towards London stopped at an unexpected red light. The driver got out to investigate and found the telephone cable had been cut. As he made his way back to the train in the dark, he was attacked from behind. The gang of fifteen moved the train and then unloaded the equivalent of millions in today's money, before returning to their hideout an hour or so before first light. It's no coincidence, of course, that this crime, known as the Great Train Robbery, was carried out at night. Those who commit theft or assault do not operate in the daylight, but under the cover of darkness.

There is something within every human heart that appreciates the cover of darkness while recoiling from the light. The person who is doing something wrong does not want that illuminated. We might not be robbing trains, but there are things in each of our lives that we would rather not be exposed to the light. Each one of us would prefer some aspects of what we do and think to stay covered up rather than revealed for all to see. Jesus explains that the world collectively—all of humanity, naturally sinful and in opposition to God—preferred the darkness, and so did not welcome the light.

Of course, we know that Jesus is right. Perhaps you personally are holding back from accepting Jesus and his message. Well, if that is you, then there is a real challenge here. You might say, "I am holding back because I am not yet convinced. I have more questions. I am weighing up different options and beliefs." It is right to search and question, but Jesus' verdict confronts you: are you actually holding back because you fear that the light of Jesus Christ will expose the dark corners of your life and actions? When you examine your heart with honesty, is that the real, underlying reason for your reluctance to follow him?

*

There is a second factor at play in why people reject Jesus Christ: there is a spiritual blindness that comes from Satan himself and prevents people from seeing the light.

We see this reality in a key statement which comes later in the New Testament:

> ... even if our gospel [message] is veiled, it is veiled to those who are perishing. In their case the god of this world [Satan] has blinded the minds of the unbelievers, to keep them from seeing the light of the gospel of the glory of Christ, who is the image of God (2 Corinthians 4:3–4).

The god of this world—Satan—works actively to blind people so that they cannot see "the light of the gospel of the glory of Christ." The light is shining and the glory of Jesus is plain to see as the good news about him is proclaimed, but some simply cannot perceive it because Satan is hard at work inflicting spiritual blindness.

It is a very cruel thing, of course, to inflict blindness on someone. It has, occasionally, been the practice of kings and rulers to blind enemies or criminals. In the eleventh century, blinding was enshrined in English law by William the Conqueror as a punishment in place of the death penalty. Some countries today still use it as a legal punishment. It is awful even to contemplate. This passage tells us that the devil makes it his practice to inflict spiritual blindness on the people of this world to keep them from seeing Christ and receiving salvation. This is the height of cruelty and malice.

It is important to know what Satan is up to. Maybe you are in that place where you want to understand the Christian message—*you sense there is something there*—but you feel you are not making progress. You see churches full of people who seem to get it, but you do not. If that is your situation, let me emphasize that there is a spiritual element to all this. There is another factor at play. And what is needed is a work of God to open your eyes and enable you to see.

With that in mind, let me now challenge and encourage you: if you feel stuck in that way, why not pray to God, asking him to open your eyes and lift your spiritual blindness? Only he has this power, and he is only too ready to hear our prayer.

*

From around five weeks, a baby's heart begins to beat in the womb. By twelve weeks fingers flex and toes curl. By nineteen weeks, all five senses are developing and a baby can hear noises outside their mother's womb. During the nine months of pregnancy a baby is continually growing and changing, and this will continue throughout childhood. But there is of course one unrepeatable event which each baby must experience—birth.

You may have heard the phrase "born again." People talk about some Christians being "born again" types. But when we pause to think about it, the very idea is strange. Being born is, by definition, a once-and-for-all event. That is the objection a man named Nicodemus raised when he visited Jesus: how can someone repeat that *unrepeatable* event? And, come to think of it, why would anyone *want* to be born again? Isn't our first birth good enough? Aren't we fully alive when we're born the first time?

Jesus' answer to Nicodemus is shocking: being physically alive does not mean that we are actually, fully *alive* in a spiritual sense. Or, as John puts it, being born of human parents does not mean that we are automatically children of God and part of his spiritual family.

You see, it is entirely possible to be physically alive, but spiritually dead. In fact, that is the reality for each of us at our physical birth. John points us to a great mystery: because the light has come, there is a work that God is ready to do in the human heart—something that he *needs* to do if we are to have life—but it is a profoundly mysterious work. He writes: "But to all who did receive him, who believed in his name, he gave the right to become children of God, who were born, not of blood nor of the will of the flesh nor of the will of man, but of God." Our first birth is not enough. Another birth is needed— one that seems mysterious to us, but which is crucially important. We need to be not just born of our parents, but born again of God himself. If we are to enjoy eternal life beyond this world—

if we are to experience life beyond the grave—
we need to be born again.

*

You and I tend to differentiate between people
on all kinds of bases and along all kinds of lines.
In our minds, we draw a line between those who
are wealthy and those who are poor; those who
are more educated and those who are less so;
those who talk and act like us, and those who
do not. We make many distinctions that we
consider important. But John wipes all those off
the table, instead giving us one simple division:
is a person born again of God or not? Is a person
a member of God's spiritual family or not?

What about me—which category do I fall into?

It is so easy to focus on our families, wealth,
education, hobbies, friendships, happiness—and
miss the most important thing about ourselves.
We might feel we are doing well in so many
areas without realizing that none of these things
ultimately will benefit us if we are still walking
in darkness and separated from the life of God.

There is another birth, a spiritual birth,
that each one of us desperately needs. There
is another kind of life that only God can

bring about. While there is something deeply mysterious about it—we cannot perceive it with our eyes or scrutinize it through science—nothing is more important.

*

The All England Lawn Tennis Club, which organizes and hosts the Wimbledon Championships, is one of the most exclusive organizations in the world. There are only 565 membership places available in total, and they almost never change hands. It is said that the *easiest* way to enter the club is to win the Wimbledon Championships—if you do that, you gain an automatic place. That is the "easy" way in because all other points of entry are even more challenging. Marrying a member of the British royal family is, I am told, the second easiest way in.

We might anticipate that membership of God's family would be a bit like these very exclusive clubs and societies. Only for the special few, the elite. Almost impossible to access.

The wonder of the Christian message is that Jesus has opened up membership to everyone. It is not dependent upon wealth, or networking, or achievement. You do not have to win a championship, or marry royalty, or have friends in high places. But you do have to receive Jesus and believe in his name. John writes: "But to all who did receive him, who believed in his name, he gave the right to become children of God."

The "name" of Jesus sums up his identity and character and message. Believing in his name means believing he has made himself known to us. Membership in the family of God is simply dependent upon accepting Jesus and taking him at his word. It is believing him to be who he says he is and believing that he can do what he has said he can do.

This is a simple but wonderful opportunity. Because of what happened at the first Christmas, this Christmas you have the opportunity to be part of God's own family. It is the opportunity of new birth. It is the chance of a fresh start. And I cannot emphasize enough how wonderful it is to be welcomed, accepted, and forgiven by him; to have security in him, for this life and the life to come.

Are you ready to receive Jesus Christ as your Lord? To submit your life to him, turning from those things that you know displease him, and seeking to follow and serve him with his help? Are you ready to believe in him, taking at face value the claims and promises of his word?

Light has come into the world. Many have rejected the light, and many reject him today. But in a profound yet wonderful mystery, new birth is offered to each of us.

This Christmas, will you receive this gift of all gifts?

THE LIGHT THAT SHOWS GLORY

And the Word became flesh and dwelt among us, and we have seen his glory, glory as of the only Son from the Father, full of grace and truth ... For from his fullness we have all received, grace upon grace. For the law was given through Moses; grace and truth came through Jesus Christ. No one has ever seen God; the only God, who is at the Father's side, he has made him known (John 1:14, 16–18).

Imagine, for a moment, that we all had lived our entire lives in one building. No one had gone out; no one had come in. The doors were sealed, and

LIGHT OF THE WORLD

the windows covered. All we had ever known was the inside of this building.

Ancient legend told us that the land in which we lived was governed by a great ruler of some kind. But none of us had seen him or her—none of us really knew anything about this ruler. We might debate among ourselves about his or her characteristics, traits, powers, and so on. From time to time we would set up public debates to discuss opinions—sometimes the conversation would be polite; occasionally less so. But essentially we would just be exchanging *opinions*, because none of us could claim to know for sure.

How could we get any real information about this ruler who lived beyond our sight and our direct experience? Well, ultimately, someone would have to walk through the door from outside and tell us.

The Christian claim is that Jesus Christ, who is God himself, has entered this world to make God known. "No one has ever seen God," says John, but "the only God, who is at the Father's side, he has made him known." Jesus came to tell us that which we could never know or discover on our own.

And when Jesus walks through the door, as it were, the debates stop. When he enters this world, speculation and opinion about God is proved worthless. We do not need to guess or imagine because now someone has come to us from the outside, to make God known.

So, what is God like?

*

I think no other age in history has seen such an interest in pursuing ultimate experiences through travel and tourism as we see now. As many nations have become wealthier, more and more people want to use their resources to seek out the most exhilarating, the most scenic, the most beautiful places—so that they can see the very best the world has to offer. They want to find something beyond the ordinary. They want to see something truly glorious. You might say that people are hungry for an experience of glory.

If we have the funds, some of us might spend vast sums pursuing this. I was reading recently about the rising trend of round-the-world cruises, not by ship, but by luxury jet. Depending on the package you purchase, for somewhere between

$100,000 and $200,000, you can buy a ticket on a specially fitted luxury jet that will transport you in indulgent comfort and splendor to some of the most breathtaking locations on earth: Easter Island, Machu Picchu, the African savannah, the Polynesian Islands, the list goes on. What a Christmas vacation that would be!

But where is ultimate glory to be found? If there are hints of glory to be seen in this world—in its most beautiful vistas and most stunning scenes—where can we find the source of true glory?

Well, it stands to reason that the creator himself would be the source and the essence of glory. The glory of his creation would be a reflection (even if a pale one) of his great glory. God is himself "glorious." And, of course, that is what the Bible tells us. When Jesus stepped into this world and was born in a Bethlehem stable 2,000 years ago to show us God, he showed us God's glory: "And the Word became flesh and dwelt among us, and we have seen his glory, glory as of the only Son from the Father, full of grace and truth."

*

When the Bible talks about the glory of God, it is speaking of his nature and character. The creator of all the earth is glorious. He radiates goodness and truth and beauty and kindness. There is something overwhelmingly bright and beautiful about him. The Old Testament makes it very clear that God's own glory was so great that even his own special people could not see it in full and survive the experience. Just as the sun is too bright, too powerful, too radiant for us to look straight at without damaging our eyes, the radiant purity of the God of heaven would consume a sinful human being.

At one point, Moses, a key leader in the Old Testament, wants to have a deeper experience of God and see his glory. Wonderfully, God allows Moses to know him in a deeper way, but he tells Moses that he cannot see his creator because that would not be safe. It would be too much for Moses to bear.

That was the situation for one of the heroes of the Old Testament. But now zoom forward to that first Christmas and to the incarnation of the Son of God: "And the Word became flesh and dwelt among us, *and we have seen his glory*, glory as of the only Son from the Father, full of grace and truth" (my emphasis). In Christ, the Word made flesh, the glory of God has now been seen in a way that was not possible in days gone by.

We all seek satisfaction, happiness and fulfilment. We try to find glory here, there, and everywhere. But only God himself is truly glorious, and so only he can satisfy. An ancient theologian once made the point that our hearts are restless in this pursuit … until they find their rest in him.

That is our reality. And John wants us to see that the God of glory has come to us in Jesus Christ. He has shown us true beauty, true purity, true wonder, true power, true goodness, true *glory*.

And somehow, as God the Son entered our world as a human being, the glory of God came to us in a way that we could see and experience and touch. God came to us in this way so that we could receive him and know him without being consumed by his radiance. Somehow, the miracle of the Son of God becoming man and dwelling among us makes it possible for us to experience what Moses never could in his day.

*

We need only look at the life of Jesus Christ as recorded for us in John's Gospel to see this glory. When Jesus performs his first miracle—the turning of water to wine at the wedding at Cana—John writes that Jesus "manifested his glory" (John 2:11). In Jesus' gracious words, in his merciful deeds, and in his powerful works, we see the glory of the creator displayed.

One of the great surprises of John's Gospel is the direction in which this theme develops as the story progresses. Later in John's Gospel, as Jesus approaches his death, he says, "The hour has come for the Son of Man to be glorified" (John 12:23). We see the glory of God in the person and work of Jesus and in his miracles, but supremely we see it as he is nailed to a Roman cross to bear the sin of a guilty people. Just like Moses, each one of us lacks the purity to stand before a totally holy God and not be consumed. We each have a catalogue of sin, guilt and shame in our lives. On the cross, Jesus displays to the world a God who is so good, so merciful, so loving that he would die to pay the price for our sin, in order that we might receive forgiveness, cleansing and life.

If the glory of God is the manifestation of his character, beauty, and goodness, then here is what John is saying: the hour when God the Son gives his life on the cross for us is the hour when, shockingly, we see most clearly the blazing glory of God.

*

We all know the fear of getting on the wrong side of the law. For those of us who generally seek to be law-abiding citizens, the place where we nonetheless fear getting into trouble is probably on the roads—letting our speed get too high, or failing to stop as we should at traffic lights.

The people of Australia now have extra reason to fear because, in addition to speed cameras and red light cameras, the police have introduced phone detection cameras in an effort to cut fatalities on the roads. These, aided by artificial intelligence, look out for drivers holding their phones and using them illegally while driving. In the first week of full operation in March 2020, the cameras reportedly caught over 3,000 misbehaving drivers in their digital net.

We all know a fear of the law and its rightful role to condemn us when we do wrong. In the

Old Testament, God gave Moses his law to teach the people how to live. Law keeping was never intended to save God's people. However, it did highlight the problem of sin very effectively. It showed people—who might have viewed themselves as essentially decent—that they did, in fact, fall short of the perfect standards of a holy God. It showed them that they needed a Savior, needed forgiveness, needed grace. We need only to read the Ten Commandments today to feel the force of that ourselves. God's holy standards highlight our sin, our failing, our guilt.

*

When the Word became flesh and walked through the door of this world, we not only saw glory, but we also received grace: "For from his fullness we have all received, grace upon grace. For the law was given through Moses; grace and truth came through Jesus Christ." What is God like? He is full of mercy and grace to those of us who know we need our guilt and sin sorted out.

For the first three months of the new system, texting drivers caught by Australia's cell phone cameras were shown grace. They received a warning letter rather than a large fine and penalty points on their license. To begin with, there was some leniency. We might think this is how God works now—choosing to look the other way when we sin and giving us a second chance, giving a warning rather than a penalty on our first offence. Is it that the God of the New Testament is a bit softer and more forgiving than the God of the Old—now extending a bit of Christmas goodwill?

No, that is not what the Bible teaches us. The eternal God does not change. His standards of holiness and justice do not evolve over time or morph with culture. But in the coming of Jesus, something else happened.

The God of holiness and grace had always planned to make a way for sinners to be cleansed and for law breakers to be forgiven. His strategy was never to sweep evil under the carpet or to ignore wrongdoing. Instead, remarkably, his plan was to pay the debt and clear the record himself: "For the law was given through Moses; grace and truth came through Jesus Christ."

God's penalty for sin—his set price for all wrongdoing and evil—has always been death itself. When the first humans, Adam and Eve, rebelled against him, he told them that they would die. And die they did. Humanity has been living under that death sentence ever since.

Ultimately, though, the God of goodness and grace always intended to pay that bill himself. But how could God show grace and bear sin's penalty of death instead of the creatures?

Here is the answer: "the Word became flesh." The eternal God, in the person of his Son, *became* human. He became what he had not been— human—so that he could do what he could not have done before—die. For, in his flesh, Jesus the Son of God could die to pay the penalty of our sin. He died under God's judgement in our place—we need only ask for his forgiveness, "receive him … [and] believe in his name."

Two thousand years ago at Christmas, the Son of God entered our world from outside, bringing truth, glory and grace. He came into this world and submitted himself to death on our behalf. He died so that he might rise, proving himself to have access to power far greater than any in this world—even power over the grave. On the first Easter morning, Jesus Christ walked out of the tomb, having beaten both sin and death. He then went back again to heaven, the place from which he came. And one day he will return.

Here is the man from outside. Here is God himself.

And if we want to know what is really true, we must listen to the Word himself. If we want to know what God the Father is like, we must look to God the Son. If we want to satisfy our longing for glory, we must set our eyes upon the One who brought light into the world. If we want to know grace and forgiveness, we must receive the Savior who came.

*

Although lots of people love Christmastime, there are not many who would opt for never-ending festivities. As we move into the New Year, Christmas trees and ornaments get packed away, leftovers get eaten or thrown out, and life returns to normal.

It is tempting to leave thoughts of Jesus Christ behind too. I would urge you not to make that mistake. Our need for grace and truth does not fade as we return to work and as New Year resolutions are made and broken. The same Jesus Christ, who existed since the beginning and was born in the stable, is alive now and seated in heaven on high. The question for you now is simply this: Will you receive him? He invites you to do so this Christmas. And if you will receive him, he promises you a new start and a place in the family of God.

> But to all who did receive him, who believed in his name, he gave the right to become children of God, who were born, not of blood nor of the will of the flesh nor of the will of man, but of God (John 1:12–13).

If you would like to respond to the invitation of Jesus, you can do so by using the words of this prayer:

> Lord Jesus Christ, I am sorry that I have chosen to live in darkness in my thoughts, actions and words. Thank you that you, the Son of God, came into the world to bring light to our darkness. Thank you that you have shown me the way to the Father, and have died in my place, so that I might be forgiven and come to him. Please cleanse me, give me new birth, and help me now to walk in the light as your follower. Amen.

Publishing